One Potato

VOYAGER BOOKS
HARCOURT, INC.
San Diego   New York   London

One Potato

A COUNTING BOOK OF POTATO PRINTS

DIANA POMEROY

With special thanks to my parents,
Annabel and Jack McIntosh, for their love
and support; my friend Gwendolyn Brusca;
and my editor, Liz Bicknell

Requests for permission to make copies of any part of the work
should be mailed to: Permissions Department, Harcourt, Inc.,
6277 Sea Harbor Drive, Orlando, Florida 32887-6777.

First Voyager Books edition 2000
Voyager Books is a registered trademark of Harcourt, Inc.

The Library of Congress has cataloged the hardcover edition as follows:
Pomeroy, Diana.
One potato: a counting book of potato prints/by Diana Pomeroy.
p.   cm.
Summary: A counting book which uses images of fruits and vegetables
to illustrate numbers from one to one hundred and which also includes
an explanation of how to do potato printing.
1. Counting—Juvenile literature. 2. Potato printing—Juvenile literature.
[1. Counting. 2. Potato printing. 3. Relief printing. 4. Handicraft.]
I. Title.
QA113.P66   1996   513.2 11—dc20   [E]   95-10986
ISBN 0-15-200300-2

ISBN 0-15-202330-5 pb

Printed in Singapore

A C E F D B

The illustrations in this book were done with
50-count potatoes and acrylic paints on Sundance Felt paper.
The display and text type were set in Saint Albans.
Color separations by Bright Arts, Ltd., Singapore
Printed and bound by Tien Wah Press, Singapore
This book was printed on Arctic matte paper.
Production supervision by Stanley Redfern
Designed by Linda Lockowitz

For my son, Bristol;
and all the potatoes
I have yet to meet

1
One
potato

2
Two eggplants

3 Three
ears of corn

Four pears 4

5 Five carrots

6 Six
tomatoes

7 Seven
oranges

8 Eight
strawberries

9 Nine turnips

10

Ten cherries

20

Twenty

radishes

Thirty
blueberries

30

40 Forty grapes

Fifty
blackberries

100

One
hundred
sunflower
seeds

Potato Printing

THE PICTURES IN THIS BOOK were made with potatoes. Potato printing is a fun, unique method of printing that can easily be done at home. Children who are too young to use a sharp knife should have a grown-up do the carving, but the children can tell the grown-up what to carve, choose the colors, and do the stamping.

You will need:
- potatoes (large, firm ones are best)
- a sharp whittling knife
- an old cotton cloth (a washcloth works well)
- small paintbrushes
- acrylic paints
- paper for printing (some smooth, some textured)

Pick a nice, firm potato that's comfortable to hold in the hand. Baking or large red rose potatoes are perfect. The potato should be smooth to the touch, without too many knots or lumps.

Cut the potato in half lengthwise to obtain the largest surface area possible ("the face"). Wipe the face with the cotton cloth to remove any excess moisture. Brush some paint on the face—now you're ready to start carving.

Start with a simple design. When I began potato printing, I printed triangles, circles, squares, and small trees on big sheets of butcher paper to make Christmas wrap.

With the knife, cut the outline of a shape into the potato face—start with a triangle, for example. After each knife stroke, rub the painted surface of the potato with your thumb. This way you can see the shape of your carving grow. Your thumb is like a windshield wiper—it pushes aside moisture so you can see better.

Once your triangle shape is outlined, start cutting away the rest of the potato to leave the triangle standing alone, in relief. You need to cut away the meat of the potato from the outside of your triangle about half an inch deep all around. Once this is done, your first stamp is ready for paint.

Dip your paintbrush in the paint and paint the triangle any color you like. The paint should be fairly thick (don't water it down) in order to hold the image. Place the painted triangle face down on the paper, putting even pressure on the potato with the palm of your hand. Press firmly and lift up. Voilà! Your first potato stamp!

You can then repeat the stamping process, printing the triangles side by side or overlapping them, using the same color paint or different ones, making your own design.

As you get more experience, you can carve and stamp more complicated shapes out of a single potato, and you can use different color shading on the same stamp to obtain different effects. You can also carve line designs into the surface of the stamp for texture.

In addition to stamping on paper, you can print on fabric—cotton and muslin work well, as do canvas and linen. In general, a fairly absorbent, slightly textured surface works best.

You can make greeting cards, gift wrap, dollhouse wallpaper, or a frieze for your wall. You can decorate clothes—or make a book!

All the designs in this book grew out of this simple method, using the lowly but lovely potato.